swaps

written by Marie Birkinshaw

illustrated by Peter Stevenson

3

Here are
some boys.

Here are some
football fans.

Here are some
football players.

Here are
some shops.

Here are some
football books.

Here are some
football stickers.

Swap you!

Just right!

written by Lorraine Horsley
illustrated by Amanda Wood

Too big,

too small,

just right for me.

Too big,

too small,

just right for me.

Too big,

too small,

just right for me.

Too big, too small.

This is just right
for me!

Good day,
bad day!

written by Lorraine Horsley
illustrated by Toni Goffe

Good boy,

bad boy!

Good girl,

bad girl!

21

Good baby,

bad baby!

Good cat,

bad cat!

Good dog,

bad dog!

Good day,

bad day!

Good night!

Purr-fect
puss

written by Lorraine Horsley
illustrated by Paula Martyr

I'm happy.

I'm sad.

I'm good.

I'm bad.

I'm cold.

I'm hot.

I'm hungry.

Now I'm not!

New words introduced in this book

cat

good

bad

cold

hot

happy

sad

hungry

are, for, here, just, not, n

Purr-fect puss

Enjoy reading this rhyme to your child. He may
remember that he has met the words 'good' and 'bad'
in *Good day, bad day!* The rhyme will help your child to
guess – and then to remember – what the words are.
It also introduces the contraction *I'm* instead of *I am*.

New words

These are the words that help to tell the stories and
rhymes in this book. Try looking at the
book again to find some of the words.
(Vocabulary used in the
titles of the stories
is not listed.)

Read with Ladybird

Read with Ladybird has been written to help you to help your child:

- to take the first steps in reading
- to improve early reading progress
- to gain confidence

Main Features

- **Several stories and rhymes in each book**

This means that there is not too much for you and your child to read in one go.

- **Rhyme and rhythm**

Read with Ladybird uses rhymes or stories with a rhythm to help your child to predict and memorise new words.

- **Gradual introduction and repetition of key words**

Read with Ladybird introduces and repeats the 100 most frequently used words in the English language.

- **Compatible with school reading schemes**

The key words that your child will learn are compatible with the word lists that are used in schools. This means that you can be confident that practising at home will support work done at school.

- **Information pullout**

Use this pullout to understand more about how you can use each story to help your child to learn to read.

But the most important feature of **Read with Ladybird** is for you and your child to have fun sharing the stories and rhymes with each other.